homes
indor

cooking

William W. Wongso and Hayatinufus A.L. Tobing

Cook all your favorite Indonesian dishes—like Chicken Satay, Pecel, Soto Ayam Madura and Grilled Chicken Sundanese Style— using these authentic, easy-to-follow homestyle recipes.

PERIPLUS

Basic Indonesian Ingredients

Banana leaves infuse a delicate flavor and aroma to foods and are used as wrappers when steaming or grilling dishes, or as little trays to hold food when cooking. Soften the leaves slightly in boiling water before use to prevent them from cracking when folded.

Candlenuts are waxy, straw-colored nuts that are ground to add texture and flavor to spice pastes and curry mixtures. Raw almonds, cashews or macadamia nuts may be substituted.

Cardamom pods are used to flavor curries and desserts—giving foods a heady, sweet scent. The fibrous, straw-colored pods enclose 15–20 pungent black seeds. The pods should be bruised lightly with a cleaver or a pestle when used whole. Do not substitute ground cardamom as it is virtually flavorless compared to the pods.

Chilies are indispensable in Indonesian cooking and many different varieties are used. The large, **red finger-length chili** is the most common and is moderately hot. **Dried red chilies** of this variety are ground to make chili flakes or ground red pepper. Tiny red, green or yellow-orange **bird's-eye chilies** are very hot and are used in soups, curries and sauces. They are also available dried.

Chinese celery is much smaller and has thinner stems than the normal Western variety, with a very intense, parsley-like flavor. The leaves and sometimes the stems are added to soups, rice dishes and stir-fried vegetables. Use Italian parsley or celery leaves as a substitute.

Coconut cream or **coconut milk** is widely used in Asian sauces and desserts. While freshly pressed coconut milk has more flavor, coconut cream and milk are now available in cans and carton packets that are quick and convenient to use. Consistencies vary from brand to brand, so use your judgment and dilute with water as needed. **Thick coconut milk** is obtained from coconut cream by diluting it by half with water; and **thin coconut milk** is half again as diluted as thick milk.

Cumin seeds are pale brown to black and usually partnered with coriander seeds in basic spice mixes. They impart an intense earthy flavor to foods. They are often dry-roasted or flash-cooked in oil to intensify their flavor.

Dried shrimp paste, known by its Indonesian name,

trasi or by its Malay term, *belacan*, is a dense mixture of fermented ground prawns that must be toasted before use—either wrapped in foil and dry-roasted or toasted over a gas flame on the back of a spoon.

Fennel seeds are larger and paler than cumin seeds, with a sweet flavor similar to anise. They add a sweet fragrance to Indian and Indonesian dishes.

Galangal is an aromatic root used throughout most of Southeast Asia, known as *lengkuas* in Singapore and Malaysia, as *laos* in Indonesia, and as *kha* in Thailand. The fresh root can be sliced and frozen for future use. It is available fresh in most large supermarkets.

Glass noodles, also known as cellophane noodles, *tang hoon* or bean threads, are thin transparent noodles made from mung bean flour. They are sold in

dried form and must be soaked in warm water to soften before use. Use rice vermicelli as a substitute.

Kaffir lime leaves are used in soups and curries of Thai, Malay or Indonesian origin. They are also thinly sliced and used as a garnish. Buy them fresh or frozen or dried—the fresh or frozen leaves are much more fragrant.

Kangkung is a highly nutritious vegetable also known as water spinach or water convolvulus. Young shoots are served as part of a mixed platter of raw vegetables for dipping in hot sauces, while the leaves and tender tips are often stir-fried.

Kencur or aromatic ginger is sometimes mistakenly called "lesser galangal" although its correct English name is zedoary. This ginger-like root has a unique camphor

flavor and should be used sparingly. Wash it and scrape off the skin before using. Dried sliced *kencur* or *kencur* powder can be used as a substitute. Soak dried slices in boiling water for approximatley 30 minutes; use $1/2$-1 teaspoon of powder for 1-inch fresh root. There is no real substitute—if you cannot find it, add more galangal and ginger to the recipe.

Lemon basil (*daun kemanggi*) is a lemon-scented herb added to dishes at the last minute to keep its flavor, or used as a garnish. Use regular basil as a substitute, although the flavor is quite different.

Lemongrass is a highly aromatic herb stalk. The tough outer layers of the stem should be peeled away and only the tender inner portion of the thick end of the stems are used. Lemongrass is sold fresh in bundles in most supermarkets.

Nutmegs are the seeds of the nutmeg tree, covered with a lacy membrane called mace. Buy whole nutmegs and grate only when needed as ground nutmeg looses its flavor quickly. Use nutmeg powder if you cannot get whole nutmegs.

Pandanus leaves are the long, thin leaves of the pandanus or screwpine palm tree. They are usually tied in a knot and boiled to release their flavor. Use pandanus essence or vanilla essence in desserts if the fresh leaves are unavailable.

Tamarind is a large, brown tree pod with a sour pulp and hard, black seeds inside. Tamarind pulp is rich in vitamin C and has a tangy, acidic taste. It is used as a souring agent throughout the world. It can be bought fresh, dried, or in pulp form, and the pulp is commonly sold in compressed blocks,

with the seeds removed. To make tamarind juice, mix 1 tablespoon of the dried tamarind pulp with 2 tablespoons of warm water, then mash well and strain to remove the seeds and fibers.

Turmeric root (*kunyit*) is similar to ginger but with a bright yellow color and a more pungent flavor. It has antiseptic and astringent qualities and stains everything permanently, so scrub your knife blade, hands and chopping board immediately after handling. Purchase fresh turmeric root as needed as the flavor fades after a few days. Substitute 1 teaspoon turmeric powder for $2^1/_2$ cm (1 in) of the fresh root.

Turmeric leaves are the large leaves of the turmeric plant that are used in some parts of Asia for cooking. They are seldom available outside Asia. Look for them in Indian food shops.

Star anise is a dried brown flower with 8 woody petals, each with a shiny seed inside, which gives a flavor of cinnamon and aniseed. Use whole and remove from the dish before serving.

Sour carambola (*belimbing*) is a pale green acidic fruit that grows in clusters on a tree. A relative of the large, five-edged sweet starfruit, carambola is used whole or sliced to give a sour tang to some soups, dishes and sambals. Sour grapefruit or tamarind juice can be used as a substitute.

Salam leaves are subtly flavored and comes from a tree in the cassia family. The taste bears no resemblance whatsoever to the taste of a bay leaf, which is sometimes suggested as a substitute. If you cannot obtain dried salam leaf, omit altogether.

Sweet Indonesian soy sauce (*kecap manis*) is a thick soy sauce brewed with molasses and sugar. If you cannot obtain it, use dark black Chinese soy sauce and add brown sugar to sweeten it.

Bird's-eye Chili Sambal

8 steamed bird's-eye chilies
1 tablespoon lime juice or
  vinegar
1 tablespoon water
$1/2$ teaspoon salt

Combine all the ingredients in a processor and blend until smooth. Serve with Banjarese Chicken Soup (page 8).

Crispy Fried Shallots

4 tablespoons oil
6 shallots, thinly sliced

Yields $1/4$ cup (50 g)
Preparation time: 5 mins
Cooking time: 3 mins

Heat the oil in a wok or skillet over medium heat and stir-fry the shallots for 2 to 3 minutes, until golden brown and crispy. Remove from the pan and drain on paper towels. Keep immediately in a sealed jar to retain crispness.

Candlenut Sambal

3 candlenuts
2-3 red finger-length
  chilies
5 bird's-eye chilies

1. Simmer both types of chilies in water for 2 minutes.
2. Gently fry the candlenuts in a dry pan until golden, then chop and place in a mortar or processor with the chilies. Grind until smooth and serve with Madurese Chicken Soup (page 24)

Fried Potato Patties (Perkedel)

500 g (1 lb) potatoes
2 tablespoons Crispy Fried
  Shallots (see above)
1 teaspoon salt
$1/2$ cup oil

1. Place the potatoes in a pan with enough salted water to cover. Boil until tender. Drain, peel, and mash the potatoes together with the Crispy Fried Shallots and salt, then allow to cool slightly.
2. Shape into 8 patties, then pan-fry in oil until golden brown.

Chicken Satay with Peanut Sauce

500 g (1 lb) chicken
  breast, cubed
24 bamboo skewers,
  soaked in water for
  several hours

Marinade
2 teaspoons tamarind
  pulp
2 tablespoons warm
  water
3 cloves garlic, peeled
4 shallots, peeled
1 teaspoon coriander
  seeds
$1/4$ teaspoon cumin
  seeds
$1/2$ teaspoon salt
$1^1/2$ tablespoons oil

Peanut Sauce
2 teaspoons oil
2–3 bird's-eye chilies
3 red finger-length chilies
3 cloves garlic, minced
200 g ($1^1/3$ cups)
  unsalted peanuts,
  dry-roasted and skinned
$1/2$ teaspoon salt
3 tablespoons palm sugar
  or brown sugar
250 ml (1 cup) hot water

Sweet Soy Dip
2 teaspoons oil
90 ml ($1/3$ cup) sweet
  Indonesian soy sauce
1 red finger-length chili,
  thinly sliced
1 teaspoon freshly
  squeezed lime juice

1 To make the Marinade, soak the tamarind pulp in the warm water for 5 minutes. Mash with the fingers and strain to obtain juice. Grind the garlic, shallots, coriander seeds, cumin, salt and tamarind juice to a smooth paste in a blender. Transfer to a bowl and stir in the oil. Add the cubed chicken, mix well and set aside to marinate for at least 30 minutes.

2 To prepare the Peanut Sauce, heat the oil in a small saucepan. Cook the chilies and garlic over low to medium heat, stirring frequently until soft, about 5 minutes. Put into a food processor with the peanuts, salt and palm sugar or brown sugar, and process briefly so that the peanuts are still chunky. Add the hot water and process again briefly to make a thick sauce. Transfer to a serving bowl.

3 To prepare the Sweet Soy Dip, combine the ingredients in a bowl and set aside.

4 Thread 4 to 5 chicken cubes onto each skewer. Grill under a broiler or over a barbecue grill until golden brown on both sides and cooked, about 5 minutes. Serve with dipping bowls of the Peanut Sauce and Sweet Soy Dip.

Serves 4
Preparation time: **35–40 mins**
Cooking time: **20 mins**

Grilled Prawn Satays (Sate Udang)

700 g (1 1/2 lbs) large
  fresh prawns, peeled and
  deveined, tails intact
1 tablespoon freshly
  squeezed lime juice
Bamboo skewers, soaked
  in water

Spice Paste
4 candlenuts, dry roasted
  until golden brown
3–4 red finger-length
  chilies
1 kaffir lime leaf, sliced
1 cm (1/2 in) aromatic
  ginger (*kencur*) or
  galangal, peeled and
  sliced
5 shallots, peeled
3 cloves garlic, peeled
1/2 teaspoon dried
  shrimp paste, toasted
2 teaspoons palm sugar
  or dark brown sugar
1/2 teaspoon salt
2 tablespoons oil
1/4 cup (60 ml) thick
  coconut milk

1 Place the peeled prawns in a bowl, toss with the lime juice and set aside to marinate.
2 To make the Spice Paste, grind the candlenuts in a spice grinder or blender briefly until coarsely ground. Add the chilies, lime leaves, aromatic ginger, shallots, garlic, shrimp paste, palm sugar or brown sugar and salt, then process to a smooth paste (add a little of the oil if needed to keep the mixture turning).
3 Heat the oil in a small pan and add the Spice Paste. Cook over medium heat, stirring frequently, until the mixture is fragrant, 4–5 minutes. Add the coconut milk and bring to a boil, stirring constantly. Simmer 2 minutes, then transfer to a bowl to cool.
4 When cool, add the prawns and toss to coat well. Set aside to marinate for at least 30 minutes. Thread 2 to 3 prawns onto each bamboo skewer.
5 Barbecue or grill the prawns for 2 minutes on each side, until lightly browned. Serve hot.

Serves 4   Preparation time: **25 mins**
Marinating time: **30 mins**   Cooking time: **15 mins**

Balinese Steamed Chicken Parcels (Tum Ayam)

700 g (1¹/₂ lbs) chicken
 breast, sliced into strips
2 teaspoons tamarind pulp
2 tablespoons warm water
2 tablespoons plus
 2 teaspoons oil
2 tablespoons minced
 shallots
1 tablespoon minced garlic
1–2 red finger-length
 chilies, thinly sliced
125 ml (¹/₂ cup) thick
 coconut milk
¹/₂ teaspoon salt
6–8 *salam* leaves or
 3 sprigs lemon basil
3 banana leaf sheets,
 each about 25 x 45 cm
 (10 x 18 in), softened in
 hot water for wrapping
 (see page 12)

Seasoning Paste

1 tablespoon coriander
 seeds
1 teaspoon black
 peppercorns
4 candlenuts
1–2 red finger-length chilies
4 shallots, peeled
3 cloves garlic, peeled
1 stalk lemongrass, tender
 inner part of bottom
 third only, sliced
1 teaspoon turmeric
 powder
2¹/₂ cm (1 in) fresh
 galangal or ginger root,
 peeled and sliced
1¹/₂ teaspoons palm sugar
1 teaspoon salt

1 To prepare the Seasoning Paste, dry-fry the coriander seeds, peppercorns and candlenuts in a skillet over low heat for 2–3 minutes until fragrant. Remove from the pan and grind to a powder in a spice grinder. Add all the other Seasoning Paste ingredients. Process until finely ground, adding a little oil if needed to keep the mixture turning.

2 Soak the tamarind pulp in the warm water for 5 minutes. Mash with the fingers and strain to obtain juice, then set aside.

3 Heat 2 tablespoons of the oil in a wok. Add the Seasoning Paste and stir-fry over medium heat until fragrant, about 5 minutes. Transfer to a plate and set aside to cool.

4 Heat 2 teaspoons of the oil in the same wok. Stir-fry the shallots and garlic until translucent, about 2 minutes. Place in a large bowl and stir in the chicken, chilies, coconut milk, salt, *salam* leaves, tamarind juice and cooled Seasoning Paste, mixing thoroughly.

5 Wrap and cook the packages according to the steps outlined on pages 12–13. If banana leaves are not available, dish the filling into an ovenproof baking dish, cover and steam for 15 to 20 minutes.

Serves 4
Preparation time: **40 mins**
Cooking time: **45 mins**

Double-wrapped banana leaf packets

The banana leaf is a versatile material that is widely used in preparing Indonesian dishes. It is frequently used to wrap foods for grilling, steaming, or grilling directly over hot coals. Almost any type of meat, such as duck, chicken, beef and even fish or eel, can be chopped, seasoned and wrapped in banana leaves to be cooked. To use, first rinse and wipe the banana leaf clean and cut it to the required sizes. Scald it with boiling water or heat it directly over a gas flame until it softens enough to be pliable without cracking. If banana leaves are not available, aluminium foil can be used, though it does not impart the subtle flavors that banana leaves do.

3 large sheets of banana leaf (about 25 cm x 45 cm/10" x 18") as main wrappers
Small strips of banana leaf for outer wrapping
1 quantity spicy chicken filling (page 10)
Wok with cover and steaming rack or steamer set

Step 1: Cut the large banana leaf wrappers into 20 x 22 cm (8 x 9 in) sheets. Cut the smaller strips 5 x 20 cm (2 x 8 in) for the outer wrappers. Place 2 tablespoons of the filling in the center of large banana leaf wrapper.

Step 2: Pleat one side of the wrapper with your index finger and press the two resulting folds of the leaf together as shown to form "wings".

Step 3: Repeat on the other side of the wrapper.

Step 4: Fold one wing from each side on the left and right to the front of the package.

Step 5: Fold the wings on the reverse side to the back of the package.

Step 6: Place the package in the center of a smaller strip of banana leaf and wrap it up around the pleats.

Step 7: Secure the top of both leaves with a single toothpick or staple the top with a stapler.

Step 8: Tuck in any open corners before steaming. Fill a wok or steamer with about 5 cm (2 in) of water. Bring the water to a boil. Place the packages on the steamer rack set inside the wok or steamer. Cover the wok or steamer and cook for 35 minutes, adding more boiling water as needed.

Seasoned Fish Fillets in a Banana Leaf

700 g (1$^1/_2$ lbs) fish fillets, sliced

250 g (2$^1/_2$ cups) grated fresh coconut

4 *daun mangkok* leaves, finely sliced (optional)

1 teaspoon salt

Few sprigs lemon basil (*kemanggi*) coarsely chopped

1 teaspoon very finely sliced lemongrass

5 kaffir lime leaves, very finely sliced

1 turmeric leaf, very finely sliced

Banana leaf squares, (15 cm/6-in across) softened in boiling water

Spice Paste

3–4 red finger-length chilies, sliced

6 shallots, peeled

1 cm ($^1/_2$ in) fresh ginger root, peeled and sliced

1 cm ($^1/_2$ in) fresh turmeric root, peeled and sliced, or 1 teaspoon ground turmeric

$^1/_2$ teaspoon salt

1 fresh lime, peeled, flesh chopped

1 To prepare the Spice Paste, grind all the ingredients in a blender until smooth. Transfer to a bowl and stir in the grated coconut.

2 Sprinkle the *daun mangkok*, if using, with the salt, rub with the fingers, rinse and drain. Add to the coconut mixture together with the lemongrass, basil, kaffir lime and turmeric leaves. Mix thoroughly, then coat the fish with the mixture.

3 Put 2 to 3 tablespoons of the fish mixture into a banana leaf square. Fold the sides over to enclose the mixture and secure the ends with toothpicks. Cook over a barbecue or under a grill for 4 to 5 minutes. Turn and cook 5 minutes or more until cooked through.

Daun mangkok are also known as *tapak leman* (Nothopanax scutellarium). The shape of the leaves is like a cup and it is usually used to cook stewed dishes. A good substitute is kale leaves or any other large, leafy vegetable leaves.

Serves 4 to 6
Preparation time: 45–50 mins
Cooking time: 10–15 mins

Fried Tofu and Vegetable Salad with Peanut Dressing

1 large or 2 small cakes
  firm tofu (250 g/8 oz)
$^1/_2$ teaspoon salt
250 ml (1 cup) oil
1 cucumber, peeled and
  sliced
200 g (1$^1/_2$ cups)
  cabbage, thinly sliced
10 lettuce leaves, coarsely
  sliced or torn
2 medium potatoes,
  boiled, peeled, and cut
  in chunks
3 hard-boiled eggs,
  peeled and sliced
Deep-fried melinjo nut
  wafers (krupuk emping)

Peanut Dressing
1 tablespoon tamarind
  pulp
$^1/_4$ cup (60 ml) warm
  water
250 g (1$^2/_3$ cups) raw
  peanuts, dry roasted,
  skins removed
2–3 red finger-length
  chilies
2 cm (1 in) fresh
  galangal root
4 cloves garlic
3 kaffir lime leaves
2 teaspoons salt
90 g ($^1/_2$ cup) palm
  sugar
500 ml (2 cups) hot water

1 Sprinkle both sides of the tofu with the salt. Heat the oil in a wok or saucepan and deep-fry the tofu until golden brown on both sides. Drain on paper towels and cut into 2$^1/_2$-cm (1-in) cubes. Set aside to cool.

2 To prepare the Peanut Dressing, soak the tamarind pulp in the warm water for 5 minutes, then mash well, squeeze and strain to obtain tamarind juice. Grind the peanuts coarsely in a food processor, then remove and set aside. Grind the chilies, galangal, garlic, kaffir lime leaves, tamarind juice, salt and palm sugar in a spice grinder or blender to form a smooth paste. Add the ground peanuts to the spice paste and pulse a few times. Add the water and pulse to make a thick sauce.

3 Put the tofu, cucumber, cabbage, lettuce and potatoes in a large bowl. Add the Peanut Dressing and toss to mix well. Transfer to a serving platter and top with the sliced egg and melinjo nut wafers.

Melinjo or *belinjo* is the fruit of a tree found in Southeast Asia (particularly Indonesia). Consisting of little but skin and a large seed (nut) inside, the seeds are ground or flattened into wafers, then dried and deep-fried as *emping* crackers (*kerupuk*). The crackers have a slightly bitter taste and are frequently served as a snack or accompaniment to Indonesian dishes.

Serves 4
Preparation time: **15 mins**
Cooking time: **30 mins**

Sweet Pineapple Curry

2 tablespoons oil
5 shallots, sliced
2 cloves garlic, minced
1 stick cinnamon
4 cloves
1 star anise pod
3 cardamom pods, slit
  and bruised
1 fresh pineapple (about
  1 kg/2 lbs), peeled and
  cut in bite-sized chunks
80 g (2/3 cup) finely
  chopped palm sugar,
2 red finger-length chilies
1 cup thin coconut milk
1 teaspoon salt
2 green chilies, sliced
  lengthwise

Spice Paste
1 tablespoon coriander
  seeds
$1/2$ teaspoon cumin seeds
$1/2$ teaspoon fennel seeds
5 shallots, peeled
2 cloves garlic, peeled
1 red finger-length chili
1 cm ($1/2$ in) fresh turmeric
  root, peeled and sliced,
  or $1/2$ teaspoon ground
  turmeric
$1/2$ teaspoon salt

1 Prepare the Spice Paste by dry-frying the coriander seeds, cumin, and fennel in a skillet over low heat until fragrant, about 3 minutes. Transfer to a blender or spice grinder and grind to a fine powder. Add the shallots, garlic, chilies, turmeric and salt to the spice grinder or blender and grind to form a smooth paste. Add a little oil, if needed, to keep the mixture turning. Set aside.

2 Heat the oil in a saucepan, add the shallots and garlic, and stir-fry over medium heat until golden brown, 1 to 2 minutes. Add the Spice Paste, cinnamon, cloves, star anise, and cardamom. Stir-fry until fragrant, 3 to 4 minutes. Add the pineapple, sugar and red chilies, and cook over low to medium heat for 5 minutes, stirring frequently.

4 Add the thin coconut milk, bring to a boil. Reduce the heat to low and simmer, uncovered, for 5 minutes. Add the green chilies and cook until the pineapple is soft, 2 to 3 minutes. Transfer to a serving dish.

Adjust the amount of sugar used according to the sourness of the **pineapple** used.

Serves 4 to 6
Preparation time: **20–25 mins**
Cooking time: **20 mins**

Pecel (Blanced Vegetable Salad with Spicy Peanut Dressing)

250 g (3 cups) *kangkong* (water spinach), washed and drained, thick ends discarded, sliced
250 g (3 cups) spinach, washed and drained
250 g (2¹/₂ cups) sliced green beans
250 g (5 cups) bean sprouts, tails removed, washed and drained
Few sprigs lemon basil
Deep-fried prawn crackers (optional)

Peanut Dressing
1 tablespoon tamarind pulp
60 ml (¹/₄ cup) warm water
2 red finger-length chilies,
1–2 bird's-eye chilies
2 cm (1 in) aromatic ginger (*kencur*) or galangal
4 cloves garlic
3 kaffir lime leaves, sliced
¹/₂ teaspoon dried shrimp paste, toasted
2 teaspoons salt
90 g (¹/₂ cup) palm sugar
250 g (1²/₃ cups) peanuts, dry roasted and skinned
500 ml (2 cups) hot water

1 Prepare the Peanut Dressing by soaking the tamarind pulp in the warm water for 5 minutes. Mash it with the fingers and strain to obtain the juice; set aside. Grind the peanuts coarsely in a food processor, remove and set aside. Grind the chilies, aromatic ginger, garlic, kaffir lime leaves, shrimp paste, reserved tamarind juice, salt and palm sugar in a spice grinder or blender to form a smooth paste. Add the ground peanuts to the spice paste and pulse a few times. Add the water and pulse to make a thick sauce.

2 Blanch or steam each type of vegetables separately in turn for 1 to 2 minutes each, being careful not to overcook.

3 Arrange the vegetables on a plate and either spoon the Peanut Dressing over the vegetables or serve on the side in a bowl. Garnish with lemon basil and prawn crackers, if using, and serve at room temperature.

If desired, use **roasted salted peanuts** but reduce the amount of salt in the dressing to ¹/₂ teaspoon. Reduce the number of chilies if desired.

Prawn crackers, or *kerupuk*, are dried wafers made from tapioca starch mixed with bits of shrimp or fish and spices, which are deep-fried until crispy then eaten as a garnish or snack. Buy them dried in plastic packets in Asian food stores. The wafers must be thoroughly dried in the oven set on low heat for 30 minutes before being deep-fried in oil for a few seconds, when they puff up spectacularly. Store fried *kerupuk* in an airtight container.

Serves 4 to 6
Preparation time: **30 mins**
Cooking time: **30–35 mins**

Mixed Salad with Coconut Dressing (Urap)

250 g (5 cups) bean sprouts, washed and drained, tails removed,
100 g (1 cup) sliced green beans
150 g (1 1/2 cups) thinly sliced cabbage
150 g (2 cups) green leafy vegetables such as *bok choy* or *choy sum*
150 g (2 cups) *kangkong* (water spinach), thick ends discarded, leaves and stems sliced

Coconut Dressing
2-3 red finger-length chilies, sliced
3 cloves garlic, peeled
2 cm (3/4 in) fresh galangal root, peeled and sliced
1/2 teaspoon ground coriander
3 kaffir lime leaves, sliced
1 tablespoon shaved palm sugar
1 teaspoon salt
200 g (2 cups) grated fresh coconut

1 Grind all the Coconut Dressing ingredients except the coconut in a food processor or blender. Transfer to a heatproof bowl and stir in the coconut. Place the bowl in a steamer, cover and steam for 30 minutes. Transfer to another bowl and set aside to cool.
2 Blanch the vegetables separately. Drain all the vegetables and place them in a large serving bowl. Add the Coconut Dressing and toss. Serve at room temperature.

If you cannot obtain fresh or frozen **grated coconut**, use dried unsweetened coconut flakes, moistened with a bit of warm water to soften.

Serves 4
Preparation time: **20 mins**
Cooking time: **45 mins**

Soto Ayam Madura (Madurese Chicken Soup)

1 chicken, quartered, or
800 g (1$^1/_2$ lbs)
chicken pieces
2 liters (8 cups) water
2 stalks lemongrass, ten-
der inner part of bottom
third only, bruised,
1 teaspoon salt
1 tablespoon oil

Spice Paste
2 teaspoons black
peppercorns
6 cloves
3 cm (1 in) fresh ginger,
peeled and sliced
$^1/_4$ teaspoon dried
shrimp paste

Accompaniments
100 g (3$^1/_2$ oz) glass
noodles, soaked in
warm water to soften,
cut in lengths
4 hard-boiled eggs,
quartered
1 portion Fried Potato
Patties (page 5)
100 g (2 cups) fresh bean
sprouts
2 tablespoons Crispy
Fried Shallots (page 5)
2 tablespoons finely
chopped Chinese
celery leaves
1 lime or lemon,
quartered
Sweet Indonesian soy
sauce, to serve
1 portion Candlenut
Sambal (page 5)

1 Place the chicken, water, lemongrass and salt in a
large pot. Bring to a boil, cover, lower the heat and
simmer gently until the chicken is tender, about
40 minutes. Remove the chicken and when cool
enough to handle, debone and cut the meat into small
cubes. Discard the bones and return the meat to the
pot. Remove and discard the lemongrass.
2 Prepare the Spice Paste by grinding the peppercorns
and cloves until coarse. Add the ginger and shrimp
paste and grind to a smooth paste, adding a little
water if necessary to keep the mixture turning.
3 Heat the oil in a wok or saucepan and fry the Spice
Paste over low heat until fragrant, 2 to 3 minutes.
Add the Spice Paste to the chicken soup.
4 Prepare the Candlenut Sambal (see page 5) and
transfer to 4 small dipping bowls to serve with the soup.
5 Divide the glass noodles, eggs, Fried Potato Patties
and bean sprouts into 4 individual serving bowls.
Reheat the chicken soup, taste and add more salt if
desired. Ladle the soup into the bowls. Sprinkle each
serving with Crispy Fried Shallots and celery leaves.
Serve with the Candlenut Sambal, lime quarters and a
bowl of sweet soy sauce on the side.

If desired, omit the Candlenut Sambal and add several
bruised **bird's-eye chilies** to the **sweet soy sauce**
instead for serving.

Serves 4
Preparation time: 35 mins
Cooking time: 45 mins

Homestyle Chicken Soup with Vegetables

$^1/_2$ chicken or 500 g (1 lb) chicken pieces
$1^1/_2$ liters (6 cups) water
1 teaspoon salt
1 teaspoon peppercorns
4–6 cloves garlic
1 tablespoon oil
1 medium carrot, peeled and sliced thinly across
2 tablespoons dried wood ear mushrooms (see note), soaked in hot water to soften, coarsely chopped

2 tablespoons dried lily buds (see note), soaked in hot water to soften, drained, hard stems removed, tied into a knot (optional)
75 g ($^1/_2$ cup) cabbage, sliced
50 g ($^1/_2$ cup) snow peas, tips and strings discarded
2 spring onions, cut in 1–cm ($^1/_2$–in) lengths
2 stalks Chinese celery, cut in lengths

8–10 hard-boiled quail eggs or 2 hardboiled chicken eggs, peeled and sliced
100 g ($3^1/_2$ oz) glass noodles, soaked in warm water to soften, cut in lengths
1 tablespoon sweet Indonesian soy sauce
2 tablespoons Crispy Fried Shallots (page 5)

1 Place the chicken, water and salt in a pot and bring to a boil. Cover, lower the heat and simmer until the chicken is tender, about 35 minutes.

2 While the chicken is cooking, grind the peppercorns in a spice grinder until fine. Add the garlic and process to a coarse paste. Heat the oil in a small saucepan, add the spice paste and stir-fry over medium heat until golden brown. Add to the soup.

3 When the chicken is tender, remove and cool slightly, then cut the meat into 1-cm ($^1/_2$-in) cubes. Set aside.

4 Add the carrot to the soup, return to the boil, cover and simmer for 5 minutes. Add the wood ear mushrooms, lily buds (if using), cabbage, snow peas, spring onion and Chinese celery. Simmer for 5 minutes until the vegetables are cooked.

5 Add the reserved chicken, quail eggs or chicken eggs, noodles and sweet soy sauce to the soup. Heat through, then serve in individual serving bowls, garnished with Crispy Fried Shallots.

> **Wood ear mushrooms** are dark-brown to black and thin and crinkly when dried. It has very little flavor and is used mainly for its firm texture and color. Use dried black Chinese mushrooms or shiitake mushrooms as a substitute.
>
> **Dried lily buds** are the unopened flowers of day lilies. They are yellow-gold in color, with a musky or earthy taste and aroma. Look for ones that are pale in color, and not brittle. Before using, cut off about a quarter inch of the woody stem at the bottom of each bud. Soak in warm water (about 30 minutes) before use. If you cannot find them omit from recipe.

Serves 6
Preparation time: **30 mins**
Cooking time: **40 mins**

Sop Buntut (Indonesian Oxtail Soup)

2 cm ($^3/_4$ in) fresh ginger, peeled and thinly sliced

1 kg (2 lbs) oxtail, cut in serving pieces

3 cloves

$^1/_2$ nutmeg, roughly broken, or $^1/_4$ teaspoon ground nutmeg

$1^1/_2$ liters (6 cups) water

1 tablespoon butter

1 large leek, bottom white part only, thickly sliced

1 large carrot, peeled and thickly sliced

2 medium potatoes, each cut into chunks

2 teaspoons salt

$^1/_2$ teaspoon ground white pepper

2–3 stalks Chinese celery with leaves, coarsely chopped

$1^1/_2$ tablespoons Crispy Fried Shallots (page 5)

1 Place the ginger in a large pot of water and bring to a boil over high heat. Add the oxtail and scald uncovered for 3 minutes. Drain, discard the water and ginger.

2 Return the oxtail to the pot and add the cloves and nutmeg. Add the cold water, bring to a boil, cover and simmer until the meat is tender, 1 to $1^1/_2$ hours.

3 Heat the butter in a frying pan and add the leek and carrot. Stir-fry over medium heat until fragrant, 3 to 4 minutes. When the oxtail is tender, add the leek, carrot, potatoes, salt and pepper to the soup.

4 Return to the boil and simmer, stirring several times, until the vegetables are cooked and the meat is tender, 15 to 20 minutes. Serve in individual serving bowls garnished with Chinese celery and Crispy Fried Shallots.

If there is less than 1 liter (4 cups) of stock left at the end of step 2, add more water to the pot when cooking the vegetables.

Serves 4
Preparation time: **15 mins**
Cooking time: **$1^1/_2$–2 hours**

29

Soto Banjar (Banjarese Chicken Soup)

1 chicken, quartered, or 800 g (1^1/$_2$ lbs) chicken pieces
2 liters (8 cups) water
125 ml (^{1}/$_2$ cup) milk (optional)

Seasonings
12–14 shallots, peeled
6 cloves garlic, peeled
2 teaspoons salt
2 tablespoons oil
^{1}/$_2$ nutmeg, roughly broken, or ^{1}/$_4$ teaspoon ground nutmeg
3 cardamom pods, slit and bruised
1 stick cinnamon
5 cloves
^{1}/$_4$ teaspoon ground white pepper

Accompaniments
100 g (3^1/$_2$ oz) glass noodles, soaked in warm water to soften, cut in lengths
1 portion Fried Potato Patties (page 5)
4 hard-boiled eggs, halved
3 stalks Chinese celery with leaves, sliced
2 tablespoons Crispy Fried Shallots (page 5)
Sweet Indonesian soy sauce, to serve
Light soy sauce, to serve
1 portion Bird's-eye Chili Sambal (page 5)

1 Prepare the Seasonings by grinding the shallots, garlic and salt to a smooth paste in a mortar or blender. Heat the oil in a sauce-pan and stir-fry the paste over medium heat, 1 minute. Add the nutmeg, cardamom, cinnamon, cloves and pepper and stir-fry for 2 minutes. Allow to cool slightly, then wrap in a small piece of muslin cloth and tie securely.

2 Put the bag of Seasonings in a large pot with the chicken and water. Bring to a boil, cover and simmer until the chicken is soft, about 45 minutes. Remove the chicken, cool, then shred the flesh. Discard the bag of Seasonings. Return the shredded chicken to the stock and add the milk, if using.

3 Prepare the Bird's-eye Chili Sambal and Crispy Fried Shallots by following the instructions on page 5.

4 Reheat the soup, then divide into 4 individual serving bowls and garnish with the glass noodles, Fried Potato Patties and eggs, spring onion, celery and Crispy Fried Shallots. Ladle the hot soup into each bowl and serve with both types of soy sauce and Bird's-eye Chili Sambal. Serve with rice cakes or steamed white rice.

Serves 4
Preparation time: 30 mins
Cooking time: 50 mins

Makassarese Beef Rib Soup (Sop Konro)

3 tablespoons oil
4 keluak nuts (*buah keluak*), cracked, flesh extracted (optional)
1$^1/_2$ kg (3 lbs) beef ribs, separated
1 tablespoon tamarind pulp
2 liters (8 cups) water
1$^1/_2$–2 teaspoons salt
2 spring onions, thinly sliced
1 tablespoon sweet Indonesian soy sauce
2 tablespoons Crispy Fried Shallots (page 5)
1 lime, cut in wedges
1 portion Bird's-eye Chili Sambal (page 5)

Spice Paste
1 teaspoon coriander seeds
1 teaspoon cumin seeds
1 teaspoon black peppercorns
4 cloves
4 cloves garlic
6 shallots, peeled
2 cm ($^3/_4$ in) fresh turmeric root, peeled and sliced, or 1 teaspoon ground turmeric

1 To prepare the Spice Paste, dry-roast the coriander and cumin seeds in a pan over low heat for 3 to 4 minutes until fragrant, then grind them together with the peppercorns and cloves in a spice grinder until fine. Add the garlic, shallots and turmeric root and process to a smooth paste, adding a little of the oil if necessary to keep the mixture turning.

2 Heat the oil in a large pot and add the Spice Paste and keluak nuts, if using. Stir-fry over low heat for 3 minutes. Add the beef ribs and stir-fry until they have changed color, about 8 minutes.

3 Mash the tamarind pulp in 60 ml ($^1/_4$ cup) of the water, then squeeze and strain to obtain tamarind juice. Add the juice, remaining water and salt to the pot, then bring to a boil. Cover, lower the heat and simmer until the ribs are very tender, about 1$^1/_2$ hours.

4 Stir in the spring onion and soy sauce, then transfer to a serving bowl. Garnish with Crispy Fried Shallots and serve with lime wedges and Bird's-eye Chili Sambal.

Buah keluak or **keluak nuts** are a kind of "nut" that is actually a seed. The oily, hard-shelled seeds resemble Brazil nuts. The meaty seeds are edible only after the poisonous hydrocyanic acid is removed by soaking and boiling them in water. Fermented *keluak* nuts become chocolate-brown, greasy and very slippery. Cooked seeds are used in a number of popular Malaysian and Indonesian dishes.

Serves 4
Preparation time: **15 mins**
Cooking time: **1$^1/_2$–1$^3/_4$ hours**

Javanese Bean Paste Beef Stew (Taoto)

1 kg (2 lbs) beef brisket,
  with some fat left on
2 liters (8 cups) water
1 teaspoon salt
$1/2$ nutmeg, roughly
  broken, or $1/4$ teaspoon
  ground nutmeg
3 cm ($1 1/4$ in) galangal
  root, peeled and
  bruised
2 *salam* leaves (optional)
2 tablespoons oil

Spice Paste
1 teaspoon black
  peppercorns
5 red finger-length chilies
8 shallots, peeled
4 cloves garlic, peeled
2 tablespoons yellow
  bean paste (*taucheo*)

Accompaniments
Boiled rice or com-
  pressed rice cakes (*lon-
  tong*) (optional)
1 portion Fried Potato
  Patties (page 5)
100 g ($3 1/2$ oz) glass
  noodles, cut in lengths,
  deep-fried until golden
  brown
10 garlic chives, or 2
  spring onions, cut into
  lengths
2–3 tablespoons Crispy
  Fried Shallots
  (page 5)
Sweet Indonesian soy
  sauce, to serve
1 lime, cut in wedges

1 Place the beef in a pot and add the water, salt, nutmeg, galangal and *salam* leaves, if using. Bring to a boil, cover, lower the heat and simmer until the beef is tender, about $1 1/2$ hours. Remove the beef and cut into bite-sized pieces. Strain the stock, discard the solids and return the meat and stock to the pot.

2 To prepare the Spice Paste, grind the pepper until coarse, then add the chilies, shallots, garlic and yellow bean paste and grind until smooth. Heat the oil in a wok or saucepan and stir-fry the Spice Paste over low to medium heat, 4 to 5 minutes.

3 Add the Spice Paste to the pot with the stock and meat, bring to a boil, lower the heat and simmer for 5 minutes. Transfer to individual serving bowls and serve with the Accompaniments arranged on a plate, so each person may add their own portions according to taste.

Deep-fry the dry **cellophane noodles**, a handful at a time, for just a few seconds until they puff up and turn golden. Do not burn.

Tau cheo, or salted fermented soybean paste, is a seasoning like Japanese miso. The sauce is sold in jars and varies from dark brown to light golden yellow in color. It is labelled "yellow bean sauce" or "black bean sauce". The basic version contains soybeans, water and salt; it is possible also to buy slightly sweetened versions, or ones with added chilli. The beans are usually mashed before being used. If you cannot find yellow bean paste, Japanese miso makes a good substitute.

Garlic chives, also known as Chinese chives, are slender green stalks that resemble common chives and are prized for their distinctive garlic flavor. Store fresh chives in the refrigerator, wrapped in paper towels and enclosed in a plastic bag. It is available fresh in wet markets as well as in supermarkets.

Serves 4 to 6
Preparation time: 30–35 mins
Cooking time: 1 hour 45 mins

Crispy Fragrant Fried Chicken

1 fresh chicken, cut into
serving portions
2 *salam* leaves (optional)
1 stalk lemongrass, tender
inner part of bottom
third only, bruised and
cut in 3 pieces
Oil for deep-frying

Spice Paste
5 candlenuts or
macadamia nuts
1 teaspoon coriander
seeds
$1/4$ teaspoon cumin
seeds
5 cm (2 in) fresh galangal
root, peeled and sliced
5 cm (2 in) fresh ginger
root, peeled and sliced
1 tablespoon turmeric
powder
4 cloves garlic
1 teaspoon salt

Serves 4
Preparation time: **15 mins**
Cooking time: **35–40 mins**

1 To make the Spice Paste, dry-fry the candlenuts or macadamia nuts, coriander and cumin seeds in a skillet or wok over low heat until fragrant, about 3 minutes. Grind them in a blender or food processor until fine, add the galangal, ginger, turmeric powder, garlic and salt and grind to form a smooth paste Add a little water if needed to keep the mixture turning.

2 Put the Spice Paste in a wok or frying pan with a lid. Add the chicken pieces and stir-fry over medium heat to coat with the Spice Paste, then add the *salam* leaves, if using, and lemongrass. Cover the pan and simmer slowly over low heat, turning the chicken pieces from time to time, until all the moisture is absorbed and the chicken pieces are tender, 30–35 minutes. Remove and discard the lemongrass and *salam* leaves.

3 Heat the oil in a wok until very hot. Add several chicken pieces, with the spices still coating the outside, then deep-fry over high heat until golden brown, about 3 minutes. Drain on paper towels and keep warm while frying the remaining chicken pieces.

The chicken may be prepared up to the end of step 2 and kept for several hours or refrigerated overnight before deep-frying.

Grilled Chicken Sundanese Style

1 fresh chicken, quartered
1 teaspoon tamarind pulp
2 tablespoons warm water
3 tablespoons oil
250 ml (1 cup) thick coconut milk
1 stalk lemongrass, tender inner part of bottom third only, bruised and cut in 3 pieces

Spice Paste

1 teaspoon black peppercorns
2 teaspoons coriander seeds
$1/2$ teaspoon cumin seeds
3–4 red finger-length chilies
5 shallots, peeled
5 cloves garlic, peeled
2 cm ($3/4$ in) aromatic ginger (*kencur*), peeled and sliced
2 cm ($3/4$ in) galangal root, peeled and sliced
1 cm ($1/2$ in) turmeric root, peeled and sliced
$1/2$ teaspoon dried shrimp paste, toasted
2 kaffir lime leaves, sliced
1 tablespoon palm sugar or brown sugar
1 teaspoon salt

1 Soak the tamarind pulp in the warm water for 5 minutes. Mash with the fingers and strain to obtain juice. Place the chicken in a bowl and work the tamarind juice into the chicken. Rub well then set aside.

2 Prepare the Spice Paste by dry-frying the peppercorns, coriander seeds and cumin seeds in a small pan over low heat until fragrant, 2–3 minutes. Grind in a spice grinder or blender until fine. Add the remaining Spice Paste ingredients and grind to a smooth paste, adding a little of the oil if needed to keep the mixture turning.

3 Heat the oil in a wok until hot and add the Spice Paste. Stir-fry over low to medium heat until fragrant, 4–5 minutes. Add the thick coconut milk and lemon-grass and bring to a boil, stirring constantly. Pierce the chicken all over with a fork and then add to the wok. Cook the chicken, turning it from time to time, until the sauce is absorbed and dries to a paste, about 15 minutes.

4 Remove the chicken from the wok, coat well with the sauce on all sides, then grill under a broiler or on a barbecue until cooked through and golden brown on all sides, 10–15 minutes.

The chicken can be prepared up to the end of step 3 and kept for several hours or refrigerated overnight before grilling.

Serves 4
Preparation time: **25 mins**
Cooking time: **35–40 mins**

Duck in Spicy Coconut Gravy

1 fresh duck, cut into
   serving portions
1$^1/_2$ teaspoons salt
1 teaspoon tamarind pulp
2 tablespoons warm
   water
3 tablespoons oil
5 shallots, thinly sliced
750 ml (3 cups) thick
   coconut milk
1 stalk lemongrass, tender
   inner part of bottom
   third only, bruised
10 curry leaves

Spice Paste
2 tablespoons coriander
   seeds
1 teaspoon black
   peppercorns
1 teaspoon cumin seeds
$^1/_2$ teaspoon fennel seeds
3 cloves
1 stick cinnamon
1 star anise pod
3 cardamom pods
3 candlenuts, dry roasted
   until golden brown,
   chopped
4–5 dried chilies, soaked
   in hot water to soften
2–3 red finger-length
   chilies
5 shallots, peeled
2 cm ($^3/_4$ in) fresh ginger
   root, peeled and sliced
1 cm ($^1/_2$ in) turmeric
   root, peeled and sliced
5 cloves garlic, peeled
2 teaspoons salt

1 Place the duck pieces in a bowl and sprinkle with the salt. Soak the tamarind pulp in the warm water for 5 minutes, then mash the tamarind and strain the juice over the duck. Rub well then set the duck aside to marinate.

2 To prepare the Spice Paste, dry-fry the coriander, peppercorns, cumin, fennel, cloves, cinnamon, star anise and cardamom in a skillet over low heat, shaking the pan frequently, until the spices are fragrant, 2 to 3 minutes. Put the spices and candlenuts in a spice grinder and grind until fine. Set aside.

3 Process the chilies, shallots, ginger, turmeric, garlic and salt to a smooth paste. Mix with the reserved spices, then add to the duck and mix so that the duck is evenly coated.

4 Heat the oil in a large saucepan or wok then add the sliced shallots. Cook over medium heat until golden, then add the duck and stir-fry until it changes color and is well coated with spices, 4 to 5 minutes. Gradually stir in the coconut milk, then add the lemongrass and curry leaves. Bring to a boil, stirring frequently, then simmer until the duck is tender and the sauce has reduced, about 45 minutes.

If preferred, you can replace the **dried chilies** with a similar quantity of fresh **red chilies**. Chicken may be used instead of duck.

Serves 4 to 6
Preparation time: 30 mins
Cooking time: 1 hour

Lamb in Rich Coconut and Spices

1 kg (2 lbs) lamb
150 g (1$^1/_2$ cups) grated coconut
$^1/_2$ nutmeg, coarsely broken or $^1/_4$ teaspoon ground nutmeg
3 cloves
2 cardamom pods, slit and bruised
1 stick cinnamon
1 stalk lemongrass, tender inner part of bottom third only, bruised
2 kaffir lime leaves
750 ml (3 cups) thick coconut milk
2–3 tablespoons Crispy Fried Shallots (page 5)

Spice Paste
1 tablespoon coriander seeds
2 teaspoons black peppercorns
$^1/_2$ teaspoon cumin seeds
3 red finger-length chilies, sliced
5 cloves garlic, peeled
2 cm (1 in) fresh ginger root, peeled and sliced
1 cm ($^1/_2$ in) turmeric root, peeled and sliced

1 Cut the lamb into serving pieces. Set aside. Dry-roast the coconut in a wok over low heat, stirring frequently, until it turns brown, 2 to 3 minutes. Grind in a blender until the mixture turns oily. Set aside.

2 To prepare the Spice Paste, dry-fry the coriander, peppercorns and cumin over low heat until fragrant, shaking the pan frequently, about 2 minutes. Grind to a powder in a spice grinder. Add the rest of the Spice Paste ingredients and grind to a smooth paste, adding a little of the coconut milk if needed to keep the mixture turning.

3 Put the Spice Paste into a large saucepan or wok and add the grated coconut, nutmeg, cloves, cardamom, cinnamon, lemongrass and kaffir lime leaves. Cook over low to medium heat and gradually stir in the coconut milk. Bring to a boil, stirring frequently, then reduce the heat, add the meat and simmer uncovered, until the sauce has thickened and the meat is tender, 45 to 60 minutes. Transfer to a serving dish and garnish with Crispy Fried Shallots.

Serves 4 to 6
Preparation time: **10–15 mins**
Cooking time: **1–1$^1/_4$ hours**

Beef Braised in Sweet Soy (Semur Daging)

1 1/2 tablespoons oil
500 g (1 lb) beef, cut into bite-sized pieces
1 stick cinnamon
1/4 teaspoon ground nutmeg
2 cloves
1 ripe tomato, diced
3 tablespoons sweet Indonesian soy sauce
500–750 ml (2–3 cups) hot water
1/2 teaspoon salt
1 tablespoon Crispy Fried Shallots (page 5)

Spice Paste
1 teaspoon coriander seeds
1 teaspoon black peppercorns
3 candlenuts
4 cloves garlic, peeled
6 shallots, peeled
1 cm (1/2 in) fresh ginger root, peeled and sliced

Serves 4
Preparation time: **15 mins**
Cooking time: **1 1/2 hours**

1 To prepare the Spice Paste, dry-fry the coriander seeds, peppercorns and candlenuts in a skillet over low heat until fragrant and the nuts are golden brown. Grind in a blender or spice grinder until fine. Add and grind the garlic, shallots and ginger to a smooth paste.

2 Heat the oil in a wok. Add the Spice Paste and cook over low heat, stirring frequently, until fragrant, about 2 minutes.

3 Add the beef, cinnamon, nutmeg and cloves and stir-fry until the meat changes color and is well coated with the spices, about 5 minutes. Scrape the bottom of the pan firmly to remove any dried pieces, then add the tomato, sweet soy sauce and just enough water to cover the beef. Bring to a boil, cover and simmer until the beef is tender, about 45 minutes. Place in a serving bowl and garnish with Crispy Fried Shallots.

You could add 60 g (2 oz) transparent bean-thread noodles, soaked in hot water to soften and cut into lengths, 5 minutes before the end of cooking time. Alternatively, add 1–2 cubed potatoes about 15 minutes before the end of cooking. For a vegetarian version of this recipe, replace the beef with 450 g (1 lb) firm tofu, deep-fried then cut in bite-sized pieces and cooked for only 10 minutes in step 3.

Seasoned Beef in Banana Leaf Packets

500 g (1 lb) ground beef
3 eggs, lightly beaten
5–6 sour carambola, sliced (see note below)
2–3 red finger-length chilies, seeded and thinly sliced
8 *salam* leaves (optional)
250 ml (1 cup) coconut cream
4 banana leaf sheets, each about 25 x 45 cm (10 x 18 in), softened in hot water, cut into wrappers (see page 12)

Spice Paste

3 teaspoons coriander seeds
$1/2$ teaspoon cumin seeds
1 teaspoon freshly ground black pepper
3 candlenuts or unsalted raw macadamia nuts, chopped
8 shallots, peeled
1 cm ($1/2$ in) galangal root, peeled and sliced
1 cm ($1/2$ in) fresh ginger root, peeled and sliced
4 cloves garlic, peeled
1 tablespoon palm sugar or brown sugar
1 teaspoon salt

1 Prepare the Spice Paste by dry-frying the coriander and cumin seeds in a pan or skillet over low heat until fragrant, about 2 to 3 minutes. Transfer to a spice grinder or blender and grind with the pepper and candlenuts until fine. Add the shallots, galangal, ginger, garlic, sugar and salt and grind until smooth, adding a little of the coconut cream if needed to keep the mixture turning.

2 Place the beef in a large bowl with the Spice Paste, eggs, carambola and sliced chilies. Mix thoroughly to distribute the seasonings evenly.

3 Place 2 to 3 tablespoons of the beef, $1/2$ *salam* leaf and 2 tablespoons coconut cream in the center of a banana leaf wrapper. Repeat until all the remaining filling and wrappers are used. Wrap and steam the packets as described on pages 12–13.

If using **sour carambola**, mix the slices with 2 teaspoons salt, let stand for 10 minutes to draw out some of the acidity, then rinse before adding to meat.

Serves 4 to 6
Preparation time: **35–40 mins**
Cooking time: **20 mins**

Sambal Prawns

500 g (1 lb) large fresh prawns, shells intact
3 tablespoons oil
1 stalk lemongrass, tender inner part of bottom third only, bruised
2 cm ($^3/_4$ in) galangal root, peeled and bruised
3 *salam* leaves or bay leaves (optional)
$^1/_4$ teaspoon freshly ground black pepper
200 ml ($^3/_4$ cup) thick coconut milk
$^1/_2$ teaspoon salt

Spice Paste
3-4 red finger-length chilies, deseeded
4 shallots, peeled
4 cloves garlic, peeled
10 candlenuts or macadamia nuts
1 teaspoon dried shrimp paste, toasted and crumbled
3 tablespoons palm sugar or dark brown sugar
80 ml ($^1/_3$ cup) water

1 Trim off the prawn legs with kitchen scissors, then rinse the prawns and drain. Leave the shells on.
2 To make the Spice Paste, grind the chilies, shallots, garlic and candlenuts in a blender or food processor together with the shrimp paste and palm sugar or brown sugar. Add the water and blend to a smooth paste.
3 Heat the oil in a wok and fry the Spice Paste until fragrant and the oil separates. Add the prawns, lemongrass, galangal, *salam* leaves, ground black pepper, coconut milk and salt.
4 Stir-fry over medium heat until the prawns are cooked through and the sauce thickens, about 15 minutes. Serve hot with rice.

Serves 4
Preparation time: **20 mins**
Cooking time: **20 mins**

Fish Steaks in Fragrant Coconut Gravy

4 swordfish or mahi mahi cutlets (675 g/ 1$^1/_2$ lbs) rinsed and dried

3 stalks lemongrass, tender inner part of bottom third only, thinly sliced

1 fresh turmeric leaf, shredded

70 g ($^3/_4$ cup) fresh grated coconut

2 tablespoons oil

10 shallots, thinly sliced

4–5 cloves garlic, thinly sliced

1 liter (4 cups) thin coconut milk

2 slices dried garcinia fruit (*asam gelugor*) or 1 teaspoon tamarind pulp

Few sprigs lemon basil, to garnish

Spice Paste

2 teaspoons black peppercorns

2 teaspoons coriander seeds

1$^1/_2$ teaspoons cumin seeds

1 teaspoon fennel seeds

1 small stick cinnamon

1 cm ($^1/_2$ in) fresh ginger root, peeled and sliced

1 teaspoon turmeric powder

6–8 shallots, peeled

3–4 red finger-length chilies

3 cloves garlic, peeled

1 teaspoon salt

1 To prepare the Spice Paste, dry-fry the peppercorns, coriander, cumin, fennel and cinnamon in a wok or skillet over low heat, shaking the pan frequently, until the spices are fragrant, 1–2 minutes. Grind to a powder in a spice grinder or blender. Add the ginger, turmeric, shallots, chilies, garlic and salt. Process to a smooth paste.

2 Spread the Spice Paste over the fish cutlets and sprinkle with the sliced lemongrass and turmeric leaf. Marinate for 15–30 minutes.

3 While the fish is marinating, dry-fry the grated coconut in a wok over low heat, stirring frequently, until golden brown. Grind in a blender or food processor until it becomes an oily paste. Set aside.

4 Heat the oil in a wok or saucepan. Add the shallots and garlic and stir-fry until soft, 1–2 minutes. Add the coconut, coconut milk and dried garcinia or tamarind. Bring to a boil gently over low heat, stirring constantly. Add the marinated fish and simmer, uncovered, until the fish is tender and the sauce thickens, about 10 minutes. Garnish with basil leaves and serve.

Serves 4
Preparation time: 45 mins
Cooking time: 25 mins

Fish Grilled in a Banana Leaf (Ikan Pepes)

1 whole fish (snapper, perch or bream), $^3/_4$–1 kg (1$^1/_2$–2 lbs)
1 tablespoon lime or lemon juice
$^1/_2$ teaspoon salt
2 banana leaf sheets, each about 25 x 45 cm (10 x 18 in), softened in hot water

Spice Paste
1 teaspoon tamarind pulp
2 tablespoons warm water
2–3 red finger-length chilies
1 stalk lemongrass, thick bottom third only, outer layers discarded, inner part sliced
5 candlenuts or macadamia nuts, dry roasted until golden
1 small ripe tomato
$^1/_2$ teaspoon ground turmeric
$^1/_2$ teaspoon dried shrimp paste, toasted
1 teaspoon salt
1 tablespoon palm sugar
Few sprigs lemon basil (*kemanggi*), optional

Serves 4
Preparation time: **20 mins**
Cooking time: **30 mins**

1 Clean and scale the fish, then make 2 to 3 diagonal cuts on each side. Place the fish on a plate and sprinkle both sides with lime juice and salt, rubbing it into the slits with the fingers. Set aside and allow to marinate while preparing the Spice Paste.

2 To make the Spice Paste, soak the tamarind pulp in warm water for 5 minutes, then mash well, squeeze and strain to obtain tamarind juice. Grind the chilies, lemongrass and candlenuts in a spice grinder or blender until fine. Add the tomato, turmeric and shrimp paste and grind until smooth. Transfer to a bowl and stir in the tamarind juice, salt, sugar and basil leaves.

3 Place the fish on 2 large overlapping pieces of banana leaf. Smear one third of the Spice Paste over the fish, rubbing some into the cuts. Turn and smear the other side of the fish with one third of the Spice Paste, then smear the remaining paste inside the cavity of the fish. Fold up the banana leaf to enclose the fish and secure with staples or toothpicks.

4 Half fill a wok with water and bring to a boil. Put the fish on a perforated metal dish or wire rack set in the wok well above the level of the water. Cover and steam until the fish is just cooked, about 25 minutes, adding boiling water to the wok every 10 minutes.

5 Place the fish, still in its banana leaf, under a very hot grill and cook 3 to 4 minutes on each side. Serve in the banana leaf.

If preferred, use 600 g (1$^1/_4$ lb) fish fillets instead of a whole fish; the steaming time will be reduced to about 10 minutes.

Smear both sides of the fish with the Spice Paste and fill the cavity with the remainder.

Fold the two sides of the leaves around the fish and tuck the ends underneath the packet.

Fish Simmered in Fragrant Soy (Pindang Kecap)

500 g (1 lb) white fish fillets, such as snapper, perch or bream
5 shallots, skins left on
2 cm ($^3/_4$ in) fresh turmeric root, washed, skin left on
$1^1/_2$ cm ($^3/_4$ in) fresh ginger root, washed, skin left on
$2^1/_2$ cm (1 in) galangal root, peeled and sliced
2 fresh or dried *salam* leaves (optional)
1 stalk lemongrass, tender inner part of bottom third only, bruised
60 ml ($^1/_4$ cup) tamarind juice (see note)
2 tablespoons sweet Indonesian soy sauce
2 red finger-length chilies, cut in lengths
3–4 whole bird's-eye chilies, lightly bruised
$^1/_2$ teaspoon salt
2 teaspoons palm sugar or soft brown sugar
750 ml (3 cups) water
5 small sour carambola, halved lengthwise

Marinade
1 tablespoon lime juice
1 teaspoon white vinegar
1 teaspoon salt

1 Wash the fish. Place the Marinade ingredients in a bowl and mix thoroughly. Rub the fish fillets on both sides with the Marinade ingredients and set aside.
2 Place the shallots, turmeric and ginger into a dry wok or frying pan and dry-roast them, turning frequently until browned, 8 to 10 minutes. Peel the shallots and bruise the turmeric and ginger with a pestle or the side of a cleaver.
3 Combine the roasted shallots, turmeric and ginger with the galangal, *salam* leaves, lemongrass, tamarind juice, soy sauce, chilies, salt, palm sugar and water in a wide saucepan. Bring to a boil and simmer, uncovered for 15 minutes.
4 Drain the fish pieces and discard the Marinade. Add the fish and the carambola to the saucepan with the sauce. Simmer until the fish is cooked, about 5 minutes, depending on the thickness of the fish. Serve hot with rice.

If **sour carambola** (belimbing) are not available, add the Marinade to the gravy in step 4 instead of discarding it.

Tamarind juice adds a fruity sourness to dishes. Soak 1 tablespoon tamarind pulp in 60 ml ($^1/_4$ cup) water, then squeeze and strain the mixture to obtain the juice.

Serves 4
Preparation time: **20 mins**
Cooking time: **35 mins**

Fish Braised in Chilies and Spices

1 kg (2 lbs) fish, cleaned and scaled
$1/2$ teaspoon salt
3 tablespoons lime juice
2 tablespoons oil
4 green tomatoes, sliced
1 turmeric leaf, finely sliced
5 kaffir lime leaves, finely sliced
2 stalks lemongrass, tender inner part of bottom third only, bruised
250 ml (1 cup) warm water
2 spring onions, cut into lengths
5 small sour carambola, halved lengthwise
1–2 green chilies, sliced lengthwise, seeds discarded
1–2 red finger-length chilies, sliced lengthwise, seeds discarded
4–5 bird's-eye chilies, bruised
Few sprigs lemon basil (*kemanggi*), to garnish

Spice Paste
10 candlenuts
3–4 red finger-length chilies
8–10 shallots, peeled
2 cm ($3/4$ in) fresh ginger root, peeled and sliced
2 cm ($3/4$ in) fresh turmeric root, peeled and sliced
2 teaspoons salt

1 Rub the fish inside and out with the salt and lime juice. Set aside to marinate.

2 To make the Spice Paste, dry-roast the candlenuts in a wok or skillet over low heat for 2 to 3 minutes until golden brown, then grind in a blender until coarse. Add the chilies, shallots, ginger, turmeric and salt and grind until smooth, adding a little water if needed to keep the mixture turning. Rub the fish inside and out with the Spice Paste.

3 Heat the oil in a wok then add the fish, tomatoes, turmeric, kaffir lime leaves and lemongrass. Cover the pan and cook over low heat for 2 minutes. Turn the fish over and cook for another 2 minutes.

4 Add the warm water to almost cover the fish, then add the spring onions, carambola and chilies. Bring to a boil, cover the wok and simmer for 5 minutes. Turn the fish carefully and cook until done, 5 to 10 minutes. Transfer the fish and sauce to a serving dish and garnish with lemon basil. Serve hot with rice.

Serves 4
Preparation time: 30 mins
Cooking time: 20 mins

Place the Filling on a disc of red dough then cover with a green disc and press the edges to seal.

Place a piece of pandanus leaf on top of a banana leaf then the cake and spoon sauce on top.

Rice Cakes with Sweet Coconut Filling

250 g (1$^1/_2$ cups) glutinous rice flour
50 g ($^1/_2$ cup) tapioca flour or cornstarch
Pinch of salt
250 ml (1 cup) water, or more as required
Red and green food coloring (optional)
2 pandanus leaves, cut in lengths
Sixteen 16-cm (6-in) banana leaf squares, softened in boiling water

Sweet Coconut Filling
150 g (1$^1/_2$ cups) grated coconut
75 g ($^1/_2$ cup) finely chopped palm sugar
1$^1/_2$ teaspoons sugar
Pinch of salt
60 ml ($^1/_4$ cup) water
12–cm (5–in) piece pandanus leaf, raked with a fork, tied into a knot

Coconut Sauce
300 ml (1$^1/_4$ cups) thick coconut milk
1 tablespoon rice flour
Large pinch of salt

Serves 4 to 6
Preparation time: 40–45 mins
Cooking time: 30 mins

1 To make the Sweet Coconut Filling, put the coconut, palm sugar, sugar, salt, water and pandanus leaf into a saucepan. Stir over medium heat until the sugar dissolves and the liquid dries up, about 8 minutes. Discard the pandanus leaf and set the Sweet Coconut Filling aside to cool.

2 To prepare the Coconut Sauce, combine the coconut milk, rice flour and salt in a small pan. Bring to a boil over medium heat and cook, stirring, until the mixture thickens, 2 to 3 minutes. Set aside.

3 Mix both types of flour with the salt and divide the mixture equally between 2 small bowls. Add a few drops of red food coloring, if using, to 125 ml ($^1/_2$ cup) of the water and stir this into one portion of the flour to form a soft, pliable dough. Add more water if needed. Add a few drops of the green food coloring, if using, to the remaining 125 ml ($^1/_2$ cup) water and mix with the remaining flour to make a green dough.

4 Pinch off about 2 teaspoons of the red dough, roll into a ball, then flatten it to make a circle 5 cm (2 in) in diameter. Repeat and put all pieces of the dough on a plate lightly floured with glutinous rice flour. Shape the green dough in the same way.

5 Put 1 heaped teaspoon of the coconut filling on a piece of red dough, cover with a piece of green dough and press the edges of the dough to seal. Repeat to make 16 cakes.

6 Place a length of pandanus leaf on a square of banana leaf and lay the cake on top. Spoon about 1$^1/_2$ tablespoons of the Coconut Sauce over the top. Pull the side facing you to touch the opposite side. Wrap up the parcels following the instructions on pages 12-13 but without using a second outer wrapping. Secure with a toothpick. Put the cakes in a steamer and steam over boiling water for 20 minutes. Allow to cool, then serve.

Sweet Shaved Ice with Bananas and Coconut Custard

4–6 ripe bananas,
steamed until soft,
about 6 minutes
3–5 cups crushed ice

Coconut Custard
$3/4$ cup (100 g) rice flour
1 liter (4 cups) thick
coconut milk
2 pandanus leaves, raked
with a fork, knotted
$1/4$ teaspoon salt
150 g ($3/4$ cup) sugar
$1/2$ teaspoon vanilla
essence

Syrup
125 ml ($1/2$ cup) water
100 g ($1/2$ cup) sugar

Serves 4 to 6
Preparation time: **20 mins**
Cooking time: **25 mins**

1 To make the Coconut Custard, mix the rice flour with 125 ml ($1/2$ cup) of the thick coconut milk and set aside.

2 Put the rest of the coconut milk, pandanus leaves and salt in a saucepan and bring to a boil, stirring constantly. Simmer for 2 minutes, then remove the pandanus leaves. Stir in the rice flour mixture, and simmer until the mixture thickens to a custard, about 2 minutes. Add the sugar and vanilla essence, and stir until the sugar dissolves. Set aside to cool.

3 Make the Syrup by bringing the water and sugar to a boil in a small saucepan, stirring constantly. Simmer uncovered for 3 minutes and set aside to cool.

4 Peel the bananas and slice. Divide into 4–6 serving bowls. Add some of the Coconut Custard and about $1/2$ cup crushed ice to each bowl. Top each portion with some Syrup and serve immediately.

Although the Coconut Custard is of a firm rather than pouring consistency, it becomes more like a cream when mixed with the crushed ice before eating.

Coconut Cinnamon Custard in a Pumpkin

1 small pumpkin (about
  1 1/2 kg/3 lbs), washed
4 eggs
200 g (1 1/3 cups) palm
  sugar, finely shaved
  with a knife
2 tablespoons sugar
Few drops pandanus or
  vanilla essence
250 ml (1 cup) thick
  coconut milk
1/2 teaspoon ground
  cinnamon
1/4 teaspoon salt

1 Slice off the top of the pumpkin and reserve to use as a lid. Scoop out the seeds and fibers and discard. Wash, drain, and pat dry with paper towels. Replace the lid of the pumpkin and steam over boiling water for 15 minutes.

2 Place the eggs, palm sugar and sugar in a bowl and stir until the eggs are well mixed. Add the pandanus or vanilla essence, coconut milk, cinnamon, and salt, and stir to mix thoroughly.

3 Pour the coconut milk mixture into the pumpkin, and cover with the lid. Place inside a steamer and steam over medium heat until the custard sets, 35 to 40 minutes. Remove the pumpkin and set aside to cool. Slice and serve at room temperature.

Serves 4 to 6
Preparation time: 20 mins
Cooking time: 1 hour

Young Coconut Meringue Cake

6 egg yolks
150 g ($^3/_4$ cup) sugar
$^1/_2$ teaspoon vanilla
  essence
50 g (scant $^1/_2$ cup) flour
100 ml (scant $^1/_2$ cup)
  sweetened condensed
  milk
125 ml ($^1/_2$ cup) warm
  water
Flesh of 4 young coconuts

Meringue Topping
6 egg whites
1 tablespoon sugar
$^1/_4$ teaspoon salt
75 g ($^2/_3$ cup) raisins

Serves: 4 to 6
Preparation time: 15 mins
Cooking time: 25 mins

1 Beat the egg yolks, sugar and vanilla essence together until the sugar dissolves and the mixture becomes pale and foamy.

2 Put the flour in a saucepan and gradually stir in the condensed milk and water.

3 Scrape out the soft pulp from the coconuts and add to the milk mixture. Stir in the beaten egg yolks. Cook over medium heat, stirring for 5 minutes until the mixture thickens. Transfer the mixture to a heat-proof dish.

4 Make the Meringue Topping by beating the egg whites, sugar and salt together until the mixture is stiff. Spread over the cake and scatter the raisins on top. Bake in an oven preheated to 200°C (400°F) until the meringue turns golden brown, about 15 minutes.

Young green coconuts *(kelapa mudur) have a gelatinous center, with a texture similar to a melon, which can be scooped out with a spoon. It has a fresh, fruity almost nutty flavor, not overly sweet. It is available fresh at fruit stalls in local wet and supermarkets. Canned version is also available at supermarkets.*

Index

Appetizers and Snacks

Balinese Steamed Chicken
Parcels 10

Chicken Satay with Peanut
Sauce 6

Double-wrapped banana
leaf packet 12

Grilled Prawn Satay 9

Sate Udang 9

Seasoned Fish Fillets in a
Banana Leaf 14

Tum Ayam 10

Salads and Vegetables

Blanched Vegetable Salad
with Spicy Peanut
Dressing 20

Fried Tofu and Vegetable
Salad with Peanut
Dressing 16

Mixed Salad with Coconut
Dressing 22

Pecel 20

Sweet Pineapple Curry 19

Urap 22

Soups and Stews

Banjarese Chicken Soup 30

Homestyle Chicken Soup
with Vegetables 26

Indonesian Oxtail Soup 28

Javanese Bean Paste Beef
Stew 34

Madurese Chicken Soup 24

Makassarese Beef Rib
Soup 30

Soto Ayam Madura 24

Soto Banjar 30

Sop Buntut 28

Sop Konro 30

Taoto 34

Poultry and Meat

Beef Braised in Sweet
Soy 44

Crispy Fragrant Fried
Chicken 37

Duck in Spicy Coconut
Gravy 40

Grilled Chicken Sundanese
Style 39

Lamb in Rich Coconut
and Spices 43

Seasoned Beef in Banana
Leaf Packets 47

Semur Daging 44

Fish and Seafood

Fish Grilled in a Banana
Leaf 52

Fish Simmered in Fragrant
Soy 55

Fish Braised in
Chilies and Spices 57

Fish Steaks in Fragrant
Coconut Gravy 50

Ikan Pepes 52

Pindang Kecap 55

Sambal Prawns 49

Desserts

Coconut Cinnamon Cus-
tard in a Pumpkin 62

Rice Cakes with Sweet
Coconut Filling 59

Sweet Shaved Ice with
Bananas and Coconut
Custard 60

Young Coconut Meringue
Cake 63